Godly Verses

Soar into the Heavenly Realms on wings of Prayer.

Written & Illustrated by:

J.M.R. Larman.

God Bless You Today
And
In
The
Day's
Week's
Month's
Year's
To Come.
Amen.

Jesus is Lord.
Of All The Earth.

Written & Illustrated by: J. M.R. Larman.

Copyright © Jessie Larman 2023

Second Edition: Carnarvon Art Studio 2023

All rights reserved. This book is copyright. Apart from any fair dealing for the purpose of private study, research, criticism or review, as permitted under the Copyright Act, no part of this book may be reproduced or transmitted in any form or by any means, electronic or mechanical, including photocopying, recording or by any information storage and retrieval systems without written permission from the publisher. Enquiries should be made to the publisher.

National Library of Australia

 A catalogue record for this book is available from the National Library of Australia

ISBN: 978-0-6450891-6-5 (paperback)
ISBN: 978-0-6450891-7-2 (ebook)
Distributed in Australia and Overseas by Ingram Content Group

Introduction

Author - Jessie Mabel Rosina Larman.
Nee Wyatt.

The Author Jessie Larman was born in England.
Was married in 1958 and emigrated to Australia in
1973 with her Husband Patrick Larman
and their three young children.
She is a Christian and
Naturalized Australian Citizen,
is fortunate to have Grandchildren,
also Great Grandchildren.
Was healed of an incurable disease in 1984
in Perth, Western Australia.
The Author at the moment is living in Carnarvon,
North West Australia
at her Carnarvon Art Studio.
Is involved with Writing, Art Work
plus Desktop Publishing,
Oil Painting etc.,.
....

Acknowledgements:

Scripture quotations taken from the Holy Bible,
New International Version.
Copyright © 1973,1978,1984
by International Bible Society.
Plus Old King James version of the Bible.
....

J. M.R. Larman

When I am with You God.

When I am with you God the time just goes.
To be in that Secret Place with you
Is a place that no one else knows
Full of peace and love and truth.

It's a beautiful place to sit with you Lord
A wonderful restful place
Where love and blessings are stored
A communion with you that I adore.

In the Secret Place where our hearts are one.
I can share my Soul with you God
You listen and speak to me as a Son
All of my being belongs only to you.

The time has gone as I've sat with you once more
Your peace is with us for sure.
Jesus is the key who opened the door
He is the way into my heart.

So to-day is another day here on this earth
Please let more Souls come to know you Lord.
Help them find love, peace and New Birth
In your Spiritual Realm.

This is my hearts cry God, please open the door
To everyone in need of Jesus my Lord.
The rich, the happy, the sad and the poor,
Help them come to your lovely Secret Place.

So Beautiful - Heavenly Father - You are.

*I Pray that you will enjoy some of the Verses in this book.
They have been written from the heart,
so I thought it would be good to share them.
I especially like the one about the Clown.
The photo was taken from
an ornament that I was given
which inspired me to write the Poem.
Many I am sure may relate
to the feelings of the Clown.
I have enjoyed collating and making the
Verses into a Book.
May God Bless you as you read them.
Jessie.*

*Jesus said "I am the way the truth and the life,
no-one comes to The Father except through me"
John: 14 verse 6.*

Birds of a Feather

All birds of a feather seem to flock together.
The rich get richer and the poor get poorer.
The Rich flock together for moral support
The Poor cling to each other for daily support.
Musicians Play Music, Singers Sing, Artists Paint, Authors write,
Bathers Swim, Gardener's Plant, Bishops Preach, Soldiers fight,
Lovers Love.
Where are you amongst these Birds of a Feather?
Do you bond yourself to some of the above or are you deceitful,
devious, do you flock together with unhelpful ones or do you flock
together with Godly people?
Godly people can enjoy all the good things in life whether they are
Rich or Poor.
Godly people can flock together to share the love of God,
the love of Jesus.
Being Birds of a Feather they can flock together - Sing, dance, pray,
plant, paint, love and be a Soldier in Christ's Army.
Where you at today, don't throw your life away.
Come to Jesus, be Rich in God.
In your Spirit be Rich even though in the world you may be poor or
wealthy - God sees your heart.
When hearts love The Lord then they love to Flock together
to fellowship, pray and Praise The Lord Jesus and
our Heavenly Father, who is the one and only True God.
God above all gods, Immortal, Invisible.
Our Spiritual Father in Heaven.
So -
Flock with Happiness & Joy today in what ever you choose to do.

Hello! Hello!

Hello!

Have you used the Hot Line to God Today?
The Line is Open 24 hours a day.
No Phone Bill Account will be sent to you.
The Hot Line is Prayer
you can get directly through
there is no Engaged Time.
No Waiting in Line,
no Crossed Lines to God.
So try the HOT LINE Straight through
to Our Heavenly Father,
talk to Him today.
He is waiting.
How long will He wait at the End of the Line?
To hear your Special Voice,
your Requests,
your PRAYERS,
your Faith.

When you go On Line in Prayer
you put your Faith into Action
believing that God will hear.

Then He Does Hear and Organizes for your
Prayers to be Answered.

WOW!

* AMEN *

J. M.R. Larman

God made Mothers

God made Mothers especially for us
They feed us, as babies they clean us,
somehow they love us,
each in their own way.
Mothers care for us all the days of our lives.
However old we may be
our Mothers still care.
Have you given a thought to-day to your Mother.
Have you told her you love her,
have you told her you care?
She may be quite young still
or old and grey.
But where ever you go
what ever you do she will always
be in your memory - in your heart.
She is part of you just as you
are part of the one who gave you birth.
Remember she does have feelings.
So - on the special day set aside
for Mothers, remember to pray
and ask God to Bless her.
You only have one Mother.
What ever she is like, without her
you would not be in this world.
She needs your love and Blessings.
Not just on the Special Mothers Day
but every day while she is here on this Earth.
If she has already left the Earth,
how about - holding her memory in your heart this:-

Special Mothers Day.

Lost Love

The last time you held me in your embrace
We cried and cried together,
we knew that we had to part just then
that there maybe no more time together.
So, I ponder and think of that embrace.

What was so special then of that time,
it was different from all others.
We knew that our love would always last
but you had to go - that was the way.
The way of the world in that moment of time.

We cried so together, the tears just flowed,
wet with the crying we were.
But the love was so real, deep in our souls.
Like in a time warp we were,
as the tears just flowed and flowed.

Then you were gone, I was left alone.
My heart though, was full of love,
the embrace that we shared was so special to me.
In my heart then I'm not really alone.

I know you must think of me now and then,
it wouldn't be right if you didn't.
If you are alive or if you are dead
your spirit lives on I know.
So where ever you are, please think of me now and then.

Where is that special place I long to be
In the arms of my beautiful love,
In the embrace of my beloved,
Shielded and safe from the world out there.

I know that you loved me,
Not for what I could give but truly
For who I am.

New Born Babies

Unborn Child

I am an unborn child
I can hear
I can feel
I am in a cocoon
I am in your womb
I have a heart beat
I am alive
I am real
I am your child
I have a right to be born
I am a human being
I was conceived in your womb
I want you to love me
I want you to look after me
I want to be your child
I want a Mother and a Father
I want to know you both
I belong to you
I am your responsibility
I can give you my love
I give you my life
I was alive at the moment of conception
I may be a boy or a girl
I would like you to want me
I need you
I cannot look after myself
I need your love

I am a Baby.

A New Life is in You.

You are going to become a Mother.
You are now pregnant with wonderful new life.
The baby in you is a living soul.
You now are not just a woman, you're infilled with new life.

You are carrying a boy or girl.
In the innermost parts - in your womb -
What a precious gift God has given you.
Don't let the womb become a tomb.

A tomb is a grave of someone dead.
Your baby is alive the same as you.
It has dear little arms, legs and toes.
A lovely face - does it resemble you?.

Don't be a murderer of this new life.
Your sin will be heavy on your mind.
All of your life you'll remember the child.
Please let it live, please be kind.

God will look after you.
When you allow your child to be born,
God will provide for you and your child.
If it's out of Wedlock don't listen to scorn.

People can be cruel if they accuse.
Have your child, ask for help, it's there for you.
Jesus forgives you when you ask.
Your baby needs love - it needs it from you.

Find Time to Smell The Roses

Are you so busy you cannot sit still?
Are you rushing and striving each day?
Moving around with not a minute to spare.
So, what about the Roses I hear you say.

Well The Lord made the Roses for us to enjoy.
But there never seems time to stop for awhile.
We rush here and there without even a care.
Never stopping to think that the Rose wants to share.

You ask me - What does a Rose want to share?
Well first there's it's beauty so lovely and rare,
creating a presence it would love you to know.
Also the perfume it breathes to & fro.

We miss so much in the struggles of life
if we never sit still for a moment or two.
The Rose is just one flower The Lord did create,
there are many more beauties to which we can relate.

Let us find time to smell the Roses to-day.
That really means - to find time to relax.
Live and enjoy the wonders of nature out there.
Stop for a while, don't let work be a snare.

The petals are soft, have you felt them to-day?
The perfume is exquisite, just right for each Rose.
Find time to-day to consider, the beauty the wonder
of something that grows.

Find time to wonder -

Maybe Smell The Rose.

Little One

Little one Sleeping There
Tender love divine.
Little one sleeping there
Are you truly mine?

Has God given you to Me?
Tender love divine.
Has God given you to Me?
Yes, - you're really mine!

Verse Taken from the Book - For The Kingdom of God.

She was my Friend.

She was my friend, she was my friend.
I loved her so, she was a very special friend.
The God of love has now taken her to be with Him.
The tears I've cried for her have made my eyes so dim.

But the friendship we had together will never fade,
because in my heart, she is not in the shade.
She has gone to be in that glorious light.
No more on this planet earth will she have to fight.

She can rest in Jesus our wonderful Lord
and watch in wonder as He is adored
by myriads of Angels around His throne.
She will know without doubt, that she is His own.

Being now in His Kingdom of peace and true love. -
We all can remember Gods Kingdom, each time we see a dove.
The Dove is a symbol of love and peace,
I pray Gods Kingdom will never cease.

I too can go home when the time is right.
Then I shall see my friend, what a glorious sight.
She will look so beautiful clothed in splendour,
as to Jesus Christ our Lord she does truly surrender.

Jesus said "in My Fathers House there are many Mansions,
I go to prepare a place for you."
I pray Lord God that my friend has a wonderful place
and I look forward to the day that I shall see her dear face.

She was so special to me, accepting me just as I am.
My dear God I praise you that she is with you -
Almighty God the Great I am.
The only true God, for ever and evermore,
now - and - for Eternity.

Golden Doorway

There is a Golden Doorway
a doorway of love.
That opens right up
to Gods Kingdom above.

Come through the Doorway,
walk through with me.
Through the Golden Doorway
Great Wonders we'll see.

Bright Golden and Shiny
as shiny can be,
Is the Doorway of Heaven
that is shown to me.

The Doorway is moving
backwards and forth.
With faith we can enter
with Gods love of course.

Oh! the wonders there are
through the Doorway so Golden.
It's shining with Heavenly light
and no hands are holding.

It is ever opening and closing
backwards and fourth.
Enticing and calling -
Gods saints of course.

That means us who are Christians.
So step forward and see.
Come through the Doorway
To Heaven with me

Pleasure

Pleasure is not a sin
Only when you invite the devil in.
Jesus died so that we can rejoice
So come and sing - lift up your voice.

Enjoy yourself and revel now
Jesus came to show us how
Remember at the wedding feast
He turned water into wine with ease.

This is the first miracle Jesus shows
He wants us to have pleasure, no woes.
So cast your cares upon The Lord
Our God above is truly adored.

There need be no more sin
When you allow Jesus in
You can laugh and play, rejoice be glad
Jesus, remember was once a lad.

He knew all the joys and woes.
He wants to keep us on our toes.
To dance and sing, with joy and mirth
Right where we are on this Planet Earth.

So - Pleasure is not a sin
Only when you let the devil in.
Rejoice in The Spirit, rejoice, rejoice.
The breath of God is in your voice.

Psalm: 18 v 11.

He made darkness His Secret Place.
His canopy around Him was dark waters.
And thick Clouds of the Skies.

....

You hide in the dark cloud the greatest treasure that ever could be.
Everlasting, Beautiful, so bright our eyes cannot see.
The beauty the glory the power and the joy.
The glorious brightness too bright for human eye.
No wonder you hide in the dark cloud God, veiled from our eyes.
You are so awesome, so beautiful so bright - you are eternal light.
Just a glimpse you let me see - it truly was too wonderful for me,
the colour was heavenly, so bright so pure.
No palette on earth could ever procure anything so bright with light
and so, so, pure.
No wonder you hide in the dark cloud God,
to shield and protect us from your awesome power.
Yet you give us a yearning to know you more - God.
We search for your Kingdom and look to the skies.
I praise you now that you protect our eyes from your brightness.
Your beautiful, your powerful light.
The light of the universe is there in the dark cloud,
when we come home to Heaven we will abound in your glorious,
wonderful, effervescent light, because
our earthly bodies will be shed
and our spirit bodies will be able to stand the brilliance,
the power the wonder of you God our Heavenly Father.
We shall then see, the veil will be gone from our eyes,
the Dark Cloud, will hide us then from the world,
when we come into our Heavenly Home and see your incredible,
Eternal Throne.
We shall then see as we are now seen.

The Clown.

I am a Clown with a smile and a frown
with big baggy pants and a hat.
My hair sticks out from under that hat
and my face is all painted with paint.

I tumble about and I laugh and I joke
everyone laughs and thinks that I'm funny.
and they laugh even more when my eyes are all runny.
They don't realize that it's all a great (SHAM)!

So I tumble and twist, hop, skip and jump
even run through a hoop full of flames.
everything is great fun and games.
Because a Clown should never be sad with a frown!

Inside though I'm hurting, so sad and alone.
My real self is inside the Clown.
But I must remember to laugh and not frown,
so that everyone may have their fun.

But when everyone's gone home from the party
and I'm left all alone with my thoughts,
I take off my hat and my old baggy pants,
then wash off the paint from my face.

I can then see part of the real me
that nobody really wants to know.
Every one's gone, I'm all on my own now
and no-one sees the tear-drop flow.

Yes I am a Clown, when I mix with you all
and we have great fun every minute.
But inside the outfit a real person is in it.
The clown is a Mask, a Sham!

We all love a Clown at the Circus,
we all love a Clown at a party for sure.
Everyone laughs at his painted face and hair
with his baggy pants as he tumbles and twists.

Nobody has a care to talk to him after the show.
Everyone goes on their way pretty fast,
with the Clown staying almost till last
washing his face paint off with his tears.

Next Day it's on with the Show
with a tumble and twist.
Because a Clown is a Clown - you see!

Jesus is Coming

Jesus is coming, He's coming one day,
Look forward to this and pray and pray.
Look to the Saviour of glory above.
Repent now and praise Him, ask for His Love.

Jesus is coming, He'll be here soon,
Will it be morning or afternoon?
None of us knows what time it will be
But He is sure coming for you and me.

Jesus is coming, so let us give praise,
Sing Allelujah's let the roof raise.
Angels adore Him fore ever on high
and we shall all see Him bye and bye.

Jesus is coming, so get up and sing,
Give your best praise to Jesus our King.
God up above loves us right now,
He sent us His Spirit of love to show how.

Jesus is coming, praise God above,
With His Holy Spirit be filled with love.
Be Happy and joyous, uplifted and free,
Jesus our Lord died for you and me.

Jesus is coming, He died on the cross
to save all us sinners, His life was no loss,
as He reigns now in glory in Heaven you know.
So - tell of His story and His love He'll bestow.

You Asked if Jesus is God?

Dear Child, You Asked if Jesus is God?

Well -
God is our Father in Heaven and Jesus is His Son.
So - God is Jesus' Daddy,
the same as you have a Dad.
As Jesus is now in Heaven with God His Father,
He sent His Holy Spirit
to be with us here so we won't be lonely.
(He is the Spirit of Jesus Christ).
We can talk to The Holy Spirit all the time,
whenever we want to.
The Holy Spirit helps us to pray to God.
If we want God to be our Heavenly Father
we have to ask Jesus to come into our hearts.
(Then - The Holy Spirit - comes in as well)
We can then call Jesus Lord.

So we have:-
God The Father
God The Son
    God The Holy Spirit.

All Belong together:

- Three in One -

(Three means Trinity)

...

Love Nanna Jessie xxx

Little Children Come to Jesus.

Little Children come to Jesus
He will set you free.
Free to walk and talk with Him,
share with Jesus and you will see.

You will see the Glory,
the Glory of the King.
Children dance before your God
and to The Lord Jesus Sing.

God is calling all the children,
Black and White and Yellow.
He seeks the heart of us all,
not the colour of any fellow.

Come to Jesus, come to God,
He is the one who made us all.
Jesus is so beautiful
He picks us up when we fall.

Little Children come to Jesus
He is all we need today.
Let His Holy Spirit
teach us how to Pray.

So, listen now children
to the voice of God today.
He loves us so very much
and waits especially - to hear us pray.

Lost Land of Teaspoons & Socks.

There is a Lost Land I am sure
of teaspoons and socks by the score.
Teaspoons disappear at a fast rate of knots
and everyone seems to have piles of Odd Socks.

There must be a Land far, far away.
Because these things never seem to stay.
We buy them and use them a couple of times.
Then surprise, surprise we loose them in drives.

We proudly wash our New Socks!
Peg them out carefully - pegs are good locks.
But after they're worn, they come back as - Ones.
The others, the partners, have gone to new homes.

Disappeared to the Land of the Lost
and nobody really counts the cost.
It must be in Millions or maybe in Billions.
From the dawn of Ages it may now be in Trillions.

And teaspoons you say, well!
Even Op Shops only find Odd Ones to sell.
Their partners their mates, or sets of spoons
Must all be on other Planets or on other Moons.

It's good for industry though I am sure,
Because they keep making more and more.
Teaspoons and socks, socks & teaspoons,
When we find two the same - that's a Pair - What a lovely
Surprise!

Then, when we go to Heaven above
There maybe teaspoons we cared for with Love.
And mountains of Odd Socks that were lost!
(Oh Joy - of Joy) but wait, we can't count the cost.
Because - where is the Other Odd Sock that we lost?

Pilgrims on a Journey

We are Pilgrims on a journey (birth).
We are Pilgrims on this earth.
Walking as our Saviour walked
and Talking as our Saviour talked.

We must walk & talk together,
be like Birds of a feather.
Helping each other to grow
as our Lord we get to know.

We must get to know Him better
maybe even write a letter
To that Soul He wants to save.
Come on now let us be brave.

We shall get to know Him more
as He opens up that door
to His Heavenly Kingdom here.
Step inside and have no fear.

We are Pilgrims on a journey (birth).
We are Pilgrims on this earth.
Brought together by God above.
Lets rejoice in God's love.

Walk and talk as Jesus did,
Fellowship as we are bid
through His everlasting Word.
Pilgrims through this earthly world.

Prayer is the Key.

Prayer is the Key that opens the Door of the Kingdom of God.
Prayer is the Key to Salvation
Prayer is the Key for Healing
Prayer is the Key to the Love of Jesus
Prayer is the Key that opens the door to let Jesus into our Heart
Prayer is the Key for the Indwelling of The Holy Spirit
                      to Live in our Body

Prayer is the Key to See through the Veil into the Kingdom of God
Prayer is the Key to Unlock All Doors to our Heavenly Father
Prayer is the most Precious Key that ever could be
Prayer is the Key that we must Never Lose
Prayer is the Key that Must Not be Mislaid
Prayer is the Key to use Each Day to open the Door, to Talk to God
Prayer is the Key to All Gifts stored
Prayer is the Key Now and Forever-more
                      Prayer is the Key.

    Please don't lose the Most Precious Key
Use the Key each Day and Night
The Key is easy to use when you know Jesus as Lord
The Key will never get Rusty if you Constantly Use it
The Key is irreplaceable, no other Key can open the door.

Remember the Prayer of a Fervent man accomplishes Much

Pray in the Spirit at All Times through Jesus Christ our Lord
with clean hands and a clean heart and you will see
the wonders of Heaven performed on this earth.

Prayer is the Key.

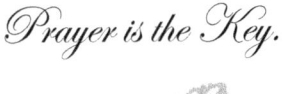

Spirit Wind Of God

Wind you are beautiful strong and so free, Wind you are lovely blowing on me.
Wind of the Spirit you blow where you will, Wind of the Spirit, Ships sails you can fill.
Where do you come from and where do you go, nobody knows as you blow to and fro.
Even though we can't see you we know you are there, as you rustle the leaves on the trees disturbing the air.
You blow gently at times oh! so gently you blow, as from East to the West you invisibly flow.
And we know as the hot air rises and rises, the birds on the thermal's fly and surprise us.
We watch in great fascination as they glide through the skies, with wings outstretched wide making circles and dives.
You are relentless though Wind - in a storm, you wail and you moan, so strong, even lifting a stone.
Not only a stone can you lift but a town, with never a smile, no never a frown.
You can be a mighty Wind when you rise, raging and roaring through the skies.
Battling the elements - snow, rain and hail, invisibly moving with a great wail.
From left to right and back again, all through the day and the night you can reign.
But when you have exhausted your mighty blast, you can be calm and gentle, even still at last.
Then we wonder where did you come from and where have you been, ears have heard you but no eye has seen.

To Belong.

What an honour it is to belong to Jesus.
To belong to The House of The Lord.
Who would think that He would even choose me?
Conceived out of wedlock, lowly and poor.
As a child I played in the gutter.
As a child I went through a war.
Was thin and sickly most of my life but since 5yrs old,
I've know Jesus as Lord through all of my strife.
Now that I'm older and able to see.
I now understand that Jesus loves me.
He has refined and refreshed me,
healed and restored now.
This servant, this creature
myself as His own - WoW!
If He can do this for me,
He can do it for you
There is only one catch -
You have to ask Him Too !!!.

Grow Strong like an Eagle.

Wait upon The Lord and Grow Stronger.
Wait upon The Lord and Grow Stronger in Spirit,
Soul, Mind & Body.
Then -
Rise up as an Eagle,
be Strong in your Faith
for
Jesus Christ our Lord.
Who Lives & Reigns - Forever
&
Ever
&
Ever
&
Evermore.
Amen.

Why Flowers God?

Why have you given us flowers God?
So beautifully soft their petals are.
The colours, such incredible hues.
Softest whites and pinks, precious as a star.

Carpets of flowers cover the earth,
we don't even have to reap & sow
because after the rains, in their seasons
the flowers burst through the earth and grow.

Some you have given to delight and please.
Some for their incredible beauty and size.
Others for perfume - aroma, so sweet.
All of them worthy of a grand prize.

Some are for healing, some just for pleasure.
They cover the earth where wild grasses grow.
Wild things of beauty, touched by no human hand.
The Petals come fourth and sway to and fro.

The stems are strong, the petals so soft.
The colours so different from species to species,
each petal so beautifully soft to our touch.
The petals are delicate, yet strong each piece is.

God do you watch the petals unfurl?
Especially the Rose Bud a Favourite of mine.
It opens up into a perfect flower
and always captures this heart of mine.

Thank you God that you have given us flowers,
to enjoy for all our days on this earth.
The beauty, the fragrance are blessings for sure
Thank you God for each flowers birth!

About Jesus.

Just over 2000 years ago
a special Baby was born.
His name was Jesus.
His Mother Mary loved Him.
His Father Joseph loved Him.
But God His Heavenly Father
Loved Him most of all.

He came to Earth
from Heaven to teach
us about God, His Heavenly Father.
And to show us the way
to go to Heaven later on.
Jesus died on The Cross for
us - He was a human sacrifice;
because He loved us so much
and wants us to be with Him in Heaven
when we leave this earth.

At Christmas time we Celebrate
Jesus Birthday, because we love Him.
(We are not sure of His real Birth date)
He was a very good man.
The best man that ever could be.
I hope I can become
a really good person like Jesus.
Amen.

What is Time?

What is time?
Time is to live
Time to die
Time to forgive
Time to try
Time to laugh
Time to cry
Time to sleep
Time to sigh
Time to eat
Time to sing
Time to pray.
Yes the time is now
To pray and praise God.
Any time is the right time
To Praise The Lord.
Time belongs to God
Time is Eternal
Time is forever
Time timeless.
Time is Time past & present
Here and now
Time waits for no one
Time is all around us
Time quiet
Time you cannot hear
Time can heal
Time you cannot feel
Time you cannot see
Time is like the wind
Time is ever present
Time has gone
Time is yet to be
Time is NOW.
...

Jesus
(You are The Prince of Peace)

You are my Saviour
You are my God
You are my Life
You are my All

You are Jesus
You are God's Son
You are The Lord
You are my All

You are True Light
You are Real Love
You are Invincible
You are my All.

You are a King
You are The Lamb
You are my Healer
You are my All

Cont'd ......

Cont'd............

You are forgiving
You are encouraging
You are Almighty
You are my All.

You are so Beautiful
You are so Comforting
You are Incredible
You are my All.

You are my Jesus
You are my Life
You are my God
You are my Everything.

(Jesus Is Lord)
He is my Lord - is He Yours?

May God The Father,
Jesus God's Son
&
The Holy Spirit be a Blessing to
you today. Amen.

Thoughts are Thoughts

Fleeting thoughts come and go,
Quickly they fade away.
Like a whisper they are gone
like a breath of air.
Quickly some come, then are gone.
Some never to come again.
Thoughts are words, words from the heart,
thoughts from our minds.
We cannot snatch them back.
Some very vivid, then gone like the wind.
Fleeting, Fleeting where has it gone?
What did it mean, how will I know
if I cannot recall?
It seemed so beautiful, a wonderful thought
and now it has gone and I know not where.
If I could catch it back in the air what
a wonder that would be.
But no, it has fleetingly brushed
through my brain like a soft brush of wings.
A fleeting thought, makes us think and wonder.
Once I was young and the thoughts stayed longer.
But now I am old and they quickly seem to fade away.
I cannot recall them so easily -
So I call them Fleeting Thoughts.
Let us treasure our thoughts while we may.
Many are precious, many are not and many are -
Fleeting thoughts soft as a gentle breeze
and then -
They are gone.

...

For Young Men & Women

What is more precious to you
to have a new boat, caravan
or to have a new baby?
To give life to a new human being
is a great privilege.
To watch them grow
to love and console,
to feed and clothe them.
What joy in your older years
to have their love and support.
The caravan & boat will
rust and decay.
But your family can be
there for you each day.
Even into old age they can be a blessing to you.
And what memories you will treasure,
of your care and love for them.
So - young people please don't abort
the wonderful life that is given.
Bring to birth another beautiful
little soul and nurture it with love.
Enjoy every moment if you can,
because God may have a wonderful plan
for the new little baby about to be born.
The more love you give the more you receive.
Don't be waylaid with money or greed.
A boat, caravan or baby what shall it be?
I chose the baby and then I had three.
What Blessings I have now that I am older.
Even Eleven Grandchildren I've held on my Shoulder.

It was a wonderful feeling -

Lord God

TO FEEL YOUR LOVE ENVELOPE ME,
WITH THE ARMS OF MY CHRISTIAN BROTHER.
TO FEEL SO SAFE AND PURE AND FREE.
YOUR LOVE JUST FLOWED FROM
ONE TO THE OTHER.
SUCH A WONDERFUL EMBRACE,
IS SOMETHING TO TREASURE,
IT IS BEYOND WORDS -

Love Without Measure

Ministry.

Dear Lord God
please Bless the Ministry
You have given to me.
That I may be a Blessing
to others.
That they will begin to see
The Lord Jesus
even through me.
Bless me still Lord
even when I do not
Comprehend the way of your Blessings.
Bless me so that I
can be a Blessing.
So that I can give
You Glory Lord God,
through Jesus Christ
my Lord & Saviour.
Bless me please Lord God,
let your Holy Spirit
flow through me.
Use me in ways I cannot see,
so that the Glory does not go to me.
Let me be a light in the darkness
for those who cannot see,
so they too may come to
the knowledge and Love of Thee.
This is my world the Kingdom of God
With Angels, Archangels - Your Kingdom of Love.
As I walk in your Kingdom God with Jesus my Lord
my Ministry is Blessed by Jesus the Word.
With my helper The Holy Spirit my Comforter and friend.

Are You a Ripple on a Pond?

Are you a Ripple on a Pond?
Do you see what I see.
Can you pray for those who cannot pray.
Will you pray for those who cannot see.

Are you a Ripple on a Pond?
Like a pebble thrown into the middle
our prayers can go out and around
in a never ending and expanding circle.

Are you a Ripple on a Pond?
Do you see beyond the horizon.
Will your words or works reach out
in that never ending circle of prayer.

I pray I am a ripple on a Pond.
My Prayers going forth throughout the world,
for those lost souls to be gathered in
and for everyone of them to be cleansed from sin.

Do try to be a Ripple,
even starting with a trickle, of Prayer and Praise.
Like a pebble creating waves on a Pond,
may your prayers go forward even beyond.

So are you a Ripple on a Pond?
With prayers, reach far beyond all that you see.
Look and use your spiritual eyes for Jesus.
Do something for Him that really, really pleases.

J. M.R. Larman

Her Name was?

A little girl has died.

She was so beautiful and kind, 13yrs old she was at the time.
Gentle and bonny - she was not mine.
She belonged to dear friends, who truly love the Lord, Jesus.
Although they grieve and mourn they know that she is in Heaven.

The Angels came and took her away.
She felt no pain - it was so quick, suddenly she just went to sleep
and moved from this world to the next.
Into Eternity she has gone to be with The Lord and God of all.
How wonderful to think that God loves us so much
that He sent His own Son to die on the Cross.

So God knows our grief He knows our sorrow.

The Mother of Jesus (Mary) watched her Son die.
Could we ever imagine her grief and cry?
When our loved ones die and leave this earth
we need to remember that God gave them birth.
We are His creatures who belong to Him.
And in God's Wisdom we have to believe that life is precious,
a gift we receive.

Cont'd on next page

Cont'd from previous page

The little child has gone back to her Maker,
her Father in Heaven, who loves her so.

She is not dead but is Risen and alive
with her Saviour, Jesus Christ our Lord in Eternity.
Where she waits with love for her family to follow,
into that wonderful lovely place of love,
Where there are no more tears of grief or sorrow,
just everlasting joy,
With Angels and Archangels in the Glory of God.

Amen.

Flowers for The Altar

So why are the Flowers on The Altar?
On The Altar of God our Father.
To show that we love Him,
to show that we care.
Flowers are so beautiful, fragile and free.
God made them all for you and for me.
He made them so soft with wonderful hues,
with Perfume incredible, reds, yellows and blues.
Beautiful Flowers full of joy and of love
perfume ascending to God up above.
Attracting the bees, the birds and insects,
each playing a part in this universe.
Birds sip at the nectar, bees collect the
pollen as part of the cycle of life.
But the beauty of Flowers especially the Rose
is far greater by far, than from the
bush whence it grows.
And we are like Flowers when we are
- Rooted in God -
Our Praise rises as Perfume.
Although that sounds odd and profane,
a Perfume surrounds us as we are Praising our God.
So look at the Flowers on The Altar!
Put there as a Blessing from us to our God,
Who made Flowers for our pleasure,
to bring joy to our hearts,
to comfort and bless us,
as we are living our walks in This life.
So - why not give a Flower for the Altar.
This treasure - this gift of a Flower is - *Alive*

They Wept.

They came and they looked and they wept.
What did they cry for?
They did not even know they were crying for their sins.
The tears just kept on flowing in a never ending stream.
They had turned their hearts to Jesus.
All their sins were forgiven.
The cleansing had started,
with warm tears streaming down their faces.
No, I am not crying they said,
"it's just water coming from my eyes."
Yes, clear clean water, living water
from The Holy Spirit.
Cleaning their souls of their sins.
After the tears the peace comes.
After the peace the joy.
God blesses His people as no on else can.
Jesus sets us free by His blood.
The blood of The Lamb on the cross.
Praise God that He loves us so much
that He sent Jesus His only Son
As the Ultimate Sacrifice for our sins.
When we accept Jesus into our life
a new life in Christ begins.
We are cleansed and renewed
by the Blood of The Lamb.
sent here to earth
by Our Father God (the only I AM).

Amen.

Message from God

This is my Will that you love my Son Jesus.
He is your Soul's life.
He abides in those who have chosen Him.
Yes, first He call's you but you still have a choice,
to choose or not to choose.
I have made you with my hands but
you are not puppets.
I desire that you choose when Jesus calls.
He knows you by name but
He will not linger where He is unwanted.
He is the Saviour of the World.
He is my only, one and only begotten Son.
And it is my Will that you would choose to follow Him
all the days of your life.
Let Our Holy Spirit abide in you to comfort and guide
you
while you live on the Earth.
Yes, Jesus has prepared a home for you in Heaven.
He is the Key that will open the door.
Only through Jesus can you come to Me.
I am the
Alpha & Omega
The first
And the Last.
I am, I AM, Almighty God
the Ancient of Days.
Come and partake of My Heavenly Realm.
Walk in the Love of
My Son Jesus.
...

The Times They Are a' Changing.

The Times They Are a 'Changing -
We have Radio, Television, Computers, Electricity.
No more Candles in Caves, we have Power for Lighting.
Power for Dishwashers, Toasters & things like Mobile Phones.
Power Point Presentations.
Times & Things are changing all around us,
Large Motorways, Channel Tunnels, Roundabouts, Parking Lots.
Trains above & below ground, plus Airplanes.
Dinosaurs are gone, many Forrest's are gone,
Times are a 'changing -
But Sunshine plus Weather Remain.
God our God, our Heavenly Father,
Jesus our Lord & The Holy Spirit are NOT a 'changing.
God is the same Yesterday & Today.
Times are a 'changing.
The World is a Wonderland of Beauty in places.
Disasters in some parts due to the Weather a 'changing.
Many of us are a 'changing,
Growing Older, Feeling still Young on the Inside
Body & Faces a 'changing with Age.
Praise God for the Changes,
He is in Charge,
Cherish each Moment Each Day as it Lasts.
Each day is a 'changing,
Different from yesterday.
Yes Times are a 'changing for You and for Me.
Praise God He is with us
& Truly can see - that -

The Times They are A 'Changing.
…..

Three In One

Water, Ice Cube, Steam.
God, Jesus, Holy Spirit.
Three in one - equals a Trinity.
You cannot have one
Without the other.
Water needs to be in all and is in all as God is.
The Ice Cube represents
The Solid Form as Jesus was the
Solid form of God when He was on Earth.
Therefore the Steam from Boiling Water
Or mist from the Frozen Ice Cube
Represents the Spirit i.e.
The Vapour - The Holy Spirit -
Who moves now in, on and around the Earth.
So when we invite Jesus into our lives
The whole three (The Trinity) are in us.

Cont'd on page 43.......

Cont'd from page 42.....

We cannot have one without the other.
Jesus sent His Holy Spirit to be
With us when He went back to Heaven.
The Holy Spirit is Invisible but Real.
Just as the Vapour from the Ice Cube
Or Steam from the kettle dissipates
And moves - So The Holy Spirit
Moves over the Earth.
Jesus sent His Holy Spirit to live
In us - to Comfort, Guide and to
Teach us about the Kingdom of God.
He is Holy, He is The spirit of Jesus.
Jesus is the Son of God (The only true Invisible God)
God is our Heavenly Father.
We belong to Him when we accept Jesus His Son.
Amen.

What to Write?

I feel ashamed of myself!
That I have nothing to Write -

How can I write anything
without the Words?
or
Without a Prayer?

How can I sing
without a Song?

How can I cook
without any Food?

How can I love
without any Love?

How can I think
without any Thoughts?

How can I run
without any Feet?

Cont'd on Page…….45

Cont'd From Page....44

How can I see
without any Eyes?

How can I hear
without any Ears?

How can I smell
without any Nostrils?

How can I praise
without my Spirit?

How can I worship
without any Holiness?

How can I live
without God's Son?

How can I bless
without being Blessed?

How can I live
Without Jesus my Lord?

J. M.R. Larman

A Night Flower

Thank you God for that absolutely
beautiful, wonderful, magnificent flower.

The bud was so big and beautiful too
and the flower only seemed to bloom about an hour.

This flower was so precious it bloomed in the night
Special for you God and hid from our sight.

Privileged I was, to go out with a torch to shed light on the bloom.
It was special for you God so glorious and white

It's petals so fragile and soft when I touched them in the torch light.
The flower gave its all as it blossomed for you God.

Because in the morning it lay limp and had gone.

One moment of Glory that most men never see
as it blossomed in the darkness and cover of night.

I shall always treasure that wonderful sight
of the beautiful flower just hanging there,
so tender and soft in the torch light glow.

Wonderful things of beauty you have made God,
they must give you great pleasure to see and behold.

Your world is so precious, your Kingdom of love,
so perfect so pure, like your beautiful dove.

Thank you Lord Jesus for allowing me to see -
the wonder the beauty of that flower.

Godly Verses

To be a Christian ✟

Dear Jesus I know I am a sinner I repent of my sins,
please forgive me and come in to my heart
to take charge of my life.
Thank you.
You are now Lord of my life,
I also acknowledge God as Father and accept your Holy
Spirit…...Amen.

…

If you pray the above Prayer and really mean it
you are immediately accepted by Jesus.
You are Born Again and belong to the Kingdom of God.
You need to tell a Christian that you have taken this step,
to speak out is an action of faith and confirms
that you have now become a Christian.

You need to begin reading the Bible.

St. John: Chapter 14 verse 6.
Jesus answered,
"I am the way and the truth and the life.
No-one comes to the Father except through me."

…

(May God Bless You With His Love.)

My Testimony

This is to let you know that The Lord Jesus Christ
Healed my lungs of an incurable disease
in 1984 in Perth, Western Australia by the
laying on of hands at a Church
Service there.
Praise The Lord for His Healing Power.
The same now as when Jesus walked upon the earth.
Also I have come to know The Holy Spirit
more fully in my life
so that The Lord God can use me
for His work and Glory.
The Holy Spirit is our Teacher,
Comforter also our Guide.
He wants us to fellowship with Him each day.
He is the one who helps us to Pray.
His presence is lovely,
once you have lived with The Holy Spirit
(who is The Spirit of Jesus Christ),
you will never want to live without Him.

...

Letter to God

Dear Lord God,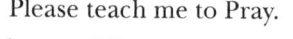

Please teach me to Pray.
As long as I live I need to Pray.
But my Prayers must be right so that your Will, will be done.
I need to be more righteous, as it says in the Bible -
"...The effectual Fervent Prayer of a righteous man availeth much"
James: Chapter 5 verse 16

Also I need faith, even as small as a Mustard Seed,
so that my Prayers will remove Mountains -
Mountains of doubt & fear, sickness, ill health, bondages & pride.
Otherwise my Prayers will not be as effective as they need to be.

Dear Lord God,

I need to Pray through Jesus Christ my Lord,
Your Son who died on the Cross
for the sin of the world including mine.

Dear Lord God,

I know also that I need your Holy Spirit to help me to Pray.
Please allow Him to teach me to Pray real effective Prayers.
So that your Will can be done on earth through the Prayers that I pray.
Let them not be selfish Prayers from my soul
but Prayers from my Spirit in line with the teaching in your

Holy Bible.

Amen.

Do not be Flippant

Let us not be flippant about The Lord Jesus.
He is the Saviour of the World.
He is God's own true Son.
Jesus is King
and Lord of Lords.
Not to be denigrated as some do.
He is to be revered and loved as our Brother,
when we accept Jesus into our lives
and God as our Heavenly Father.
Jesus is our family, we are His family.
We belong to the King of Kings.
Who is to be honoured and loved as a member of our family.
Because He is our Brother even though He is King of the World.
Let us remember that He has rescued us from sin & death.
We will be with Jesus when we die and go to Heaven.
But He is with us each day while we live on this earth
by the presence of His Holy Spirit, who He sent to be our
Comforter, Teacher and Guide.
The Holy Spirit is a beautiful companion to us
who we can fellowship with day and night.
The Spirit of Jesus is also
our Protector from the sin of the World.
He loves us with the love of God our Father and Jesus.
The Holy Spirit waits for us to communicate with Him,
talk to Him, fellowship with Him.
He will help us to Pray, to Sing, to Speak of Jesus.
So let us not be flippant about The Lord Jesus.
He is Jesus Christ _my_ Lord.
He can be your Lord Jesus too _if_ you would like Him to be.

Where is that Special Place?

Where is that Special Place I yearn to be?
In the arms of my beautiful love,
in the embrace of my beloved,
Shielded and safe from the world out there.

Who would know that in my heart
there is this longing and longing
to be accepted for who I am
not just for what I can give.
Accept me my beloved in your heart.

The world is a cold and lonely place,
Wintertime so bare and bleak.
Summer and Spring give hope,
with fluttering's of new birth.
But Autumn has a different face.

Now that the flush of youth has gone,
where are you my love my beautiful one?
I wait and hope each day for you,
longing and yearning for your love.
The remembrance of our embrace will never be gone.

Cont'd on Page 53

Cont'd from page 52

There is an awakening in my heart to-day,
I feel that you are not far away.
But I cannot see you anymore
Although your memory lingers on,
and in my heart you are here to stay.

You came into my heart when I was quite young
very naïve I was for sure,
not knowing then that you meant so much.
Taking for granted your beautiful presence,
Reveling in your joy and fun.

In the twilight I can sit and think,
of the days that have gone before
and no-one knows of the love in my heart
that I'm longing to give to you my Love.

Please Listen with your Heart.

Why do they hear and not listen.
They hear the sounds
They hear my voice
But their heart does not comprehend
The message that I am speaking.
I talk and think they are listening
But then all is lost as they speak,
Something not at all relevant to my voice.
Have I wasted my time on them?
Do they not understand
The feelings of my soul?
My soul is grieved by their response.
Where was their heart while I was speaking?
What were they thinking when they
Could have been listening?
I do forgive as they cannot comprehend
Maybe the message that I was speaking,
Or - maybe it's my fault expecting
Too much of their time to listen to me.

Cont'd on next page…

Cont'd…

What-ever the problem, it is very sad
That their heart cannot be at peace,
To listen, comprehend and show feeling
Towards my thoughts, my fears, my loves.
I am glad that you listen God, you
Know my heart, my thoughts my soul,
My longings, my fears, my loves.
To share with a human friend
Would be a comfort and an extra blessing.
As they too would receive your
Wonderful peace in their hearts,
Just for forgetting all else of the world
And listening with their heart to the
Other person pouring out their soul.

Christians as Pilgrims

We are <u>Pilgrims</u> on a journey. Many are <u>Prisoners</u> on a journey.
Help us who are Pilgrims, followers of Christ, to help those
prisoners, who are not in Christ.
We who are Pilgrims for Jesus Christ are privileged so much that
our souls are set free.
We can soar like the Eagles way, way up above
into the realms of infinite love.
We are the Pilgrims upon this earth, we who have already
had our New Birth into the Spiritual Realm of God,
the only I AM, the only true God,
our Father, our Maker, our only Liberator.
Who through the shed blood of Jesus His son,
adopts us into His Royal Family.
So we can become the Son's of God our Father in Heaven,
brothers and sisters in Christ Jesus and
friends with The Holy Spirit.
Oh! To be a Pilgrim, on this Planet Earth,
to work here for the Heavenly Kingdom.
What a privilege that God has chosen to invite
us all to become His Own.

Blessed be the Name of The Lord God
Blessed be His Holy Name.
The Name above all Gods.
Who truly lives and reigns in Heaven above with legions
of Angels and Holy Ones.
As we pilgrim on this earth we have a vision of our Heavenly Home.
Jesus we know you are coming back soon,
we want and look forward to that day.
A day when those who are prisoners in their bodies will still have a
chance to become an adopted son, of God our Father in Heaven.

Cont'd on next page....

Cont'd...

Don't delay, don't be robbed of your Royal and Holy inheritance.
Start to Pray.
The Holy Spirit will show the way,
when you acknowledge Jesus as your deliverer and Saviour.
Jesus came that all of us may be saved,
He shed His blood on the Cross for all of us,
man, woman and child, not just for a selected few.
Yes even for you, even for me.
God is Love, God is Truth, God is Eternal,
God is the Creator of this Earth - this Universe.
He sees all, He hears all. Your faintest cry of
Jesus - will be music in His Ears.
All who come to Jesus God's Son will belong to Him.

***

I am a pilgrim on this earth, I have received my New Birth,
into the realm of The Spirit I soar,
death has no hold on me, Heaven has opened it's door.
By The Holy Spirit I can transcend this earthly life,
my own spirit belongs to Jesus.
He is my Lord, my Saviour.
He is my Redeemer.
He is my all.
He is my everything.
He is the Way - the only way to The Father,
Almighty God who reigns on high for-ever and ever.

Amen.

Forgive Me
(Written after receiving a Wonderful Healing)
***

Forgive me for all the sins I've committed.
God in your goodness guide me now.
For years in the world of darkness I've been.
The light of your goodness I'd rarely seen.

But now I've been born of your Spirit.
The Spirit of Jesus - Your Son.
Your love overwhelms me each day as I live.
To God, Jesus and Holy Spirit - my body I give.

I give you my body now - healed and restored
by Jesus Christ our most wonderful Lord.
I'm healed of diseases and wrong spirits now.
So it's time to go out in Your Spirit and Sow.

Go out and sow the seed of true love,
straight from God our Father above.
Jesus is with us each day as we live.
Holy Spirit of Jesus, Gods Love help us give.

Help us to give God's love - to the poor.
The poor are the souls who have not opened the door.
Jesus our Lord is the one with the Keys.
So come pray with me, go down on your knees.

Ask His forgiveness - He wants you to.
Then listen and do what He tells you to do.
It's all in the Bible - Gods wonderful Book.
Go on, open it up - just have a look.

***

Let your Spirit Soar.

Close your eyes let your Spirit soar
into the Heavenly Realms.
Far above our humble daily chores
up above the clouds on high
far beyond our earthly sky.
Jesus our Lord and Saviour is there
surrounded by boundless love and care.
Seated at the Right Hand of God.

Who is -
Almighty God
(Father of Jesus)

the only
I AM

With Angels abounding in Glorious light.
Imagine such a beautiful sight.
Let your Spirit soar
into the Heavenly Realms.
Feel the Peace, the Love of God

As you Praise Him

in your

heart.

*H*allelujah, *H*allelujah
Hear the trumpet sound,
Jesus is Lord of all the earth.
So, we maybe standing
on

Holy Ground.
When we Pray
&
Praise
our
God
our feet
maybe Holy,
standing in the
Power of God.

Proclaiming

- *Jesus is Lord* -
of all the earth,
the sky,
the sea.

Everything
Here
that ever
could be.

God's Love

Can it be Lord, that you love me,
as I sit and wonder about Eternity?
One day I should be there
with Jesus my Lord.
Who, I know by your
Angels God - is truly adored.
Almighty God,
Ruler of the Universe,
how can it be that you think of me?
Small and insignificant
that's who I am.
Yes, you sent your Son Jesus
to rescue even me.
It is beyond my comprehension
to consider these things.
So I shall sit in
Your presence
and pray to believe
In your unconditional love.
Love full of peace.
Love without Measure.
Poured down upon us,
as we sit, stand or kneel,
in wonder and praise
at your

Glorious Presence
in Eternity.

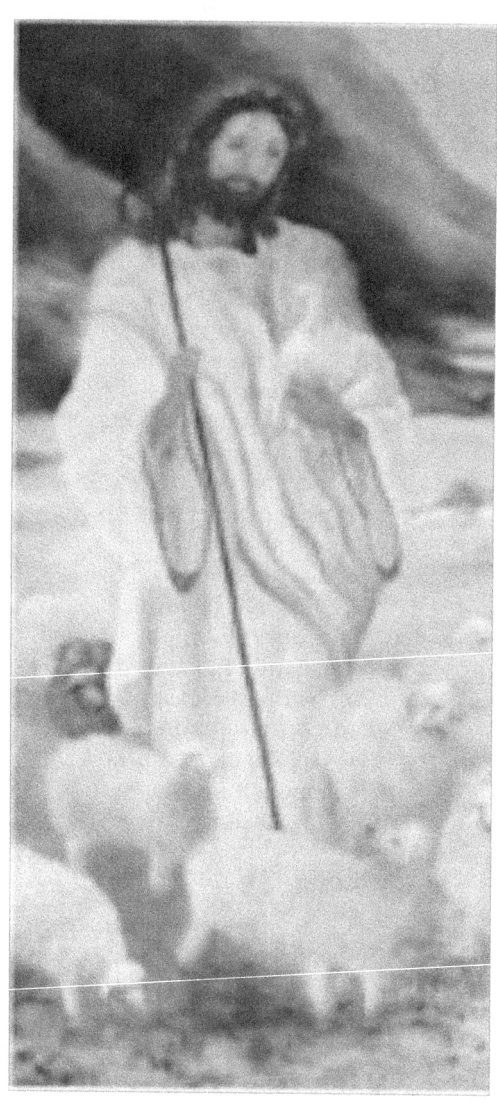

The Good Shepherd - knows His Sheep.

Index Page

Page #		Page #	
1	Introduction	29	What is Time?
2	When I am with You God.	30	Jesus
4	Birds of a Feather	31	Thoughts are Thoughts
5	Hello! Hello!	32	For Young Men & Women
6	God made Mothers	33	It was a wonderful feeling
7	Lost Love	34	Ministry.
9	Unborn Child	35	Are You a Ripple on a Pond.?
10	A New Life is in You.	36	Her Name was ?
11	Find Time to Smell The Roses	38	Flowers for The Altar
12	Little One	39	They Wept.
13	She was my Friend.	40	Message from God
14	Golden Doorway	41	The Times They Are a' Changing.
15	Pleasure	42	Three In One
16	Psalm: 18 v 11.	44	What to Write?
17	The Clown.	46	A Night Flower
18	Jesus is Coming	47	Drawing of Angel
19	You Asked if Jesus is God?	48	To be a Christian
20	Little Children Come to Jesus.	49	My Testimony
21	Lost Land of Teaspoons & Socks.	50	Letter to God
22	Pilgrims on a Journey	51	Do not be Flippant
23	Prayer is the Key.	52	Where is that Special Place ?
24	Spirit Wind Of God	54	Please Listen with your Heart.
25	To Belong.	56	Christians as Pilgrims
26	Grow Strong like an Eagle.	58	Forgive Me
27	Why Flowers God?	59	Let your Spirit Soar
28	About Jesus.	60	Hallelujah, Hallelujah
		61	God's Love
		62	Good Shepherd Picture

1st Edition Printed April 2009.
Second Edition April 2023.